# History of Canada
# Since 1867

## Robert Bothwell

*The Association for Canadian Studies in the United States*
# (ACSUS)

The Association for Canadian Studies in the United States (ACSUS), founded in 1971, is a multidisciplinary academic organization devoted to encouraging and supporting the study of Canada and the Canada-United States relationship in all its facets. ACSUS publishes a quarterly scholarly journal, The American Review of Canadian Studies, a regular newsletter, Canadian Studies Update, and hosts a biennial conference atrracting over 600 participants. ACSUS is the largest association of Canadian Studies specialists in the world.

### Also published by ACSUS:

*Northern Exposures: Scholarship on Canada in the United States*, edited by Karen L. Gould, Joseph T. Jockel, and William Metcalfe (1993) ISBN 1-883027-00-4

# Acknowledgment

The ACSUS Papers were conceived to provide suitable core materials for introductory college courses and solid background material for more focused courses on Canada for undergraduates in the United States. The first edition, published in 1989, was extremely successful in serving this market. The concept of the series has withstood the test of time and ACSUS is pleased to cooperate with Michigan State University Press on this second edition.

This edition was made possible with the assistance of the Government of Canada/*avec l'aide du Gouvernement du Canada.*

## Editors:

Joseph T. Jockel
St. Lawrence University

Victor M. Howard
Michigan State University

The study of Canada begins with a political distinction: It is a parliamentary democracy that is also a constitutional monarchy in the northern half of the continent, so its form of government is unlike that of the United States or any other countries on the American continents. The distinction derives from Canada's history, and such is the weight of that history that no serious political movement has ever arisen that sought to alter the monarchical aspect of Canada's government.

Yet the mere existence of the monarchical principle does not reassure Canadians that their country enjoys not merely a distinction but a genuine difference with the United States. So closely do the two countries resemble one another that most Canadian television can pass as American; the accents, the streetscapes, even the cultural assumptions make the differences difficult to detect. "Toronto," Peter Ustinov once remarked, "is New York run by the Swiss."

It is this blurring of identities that makes academic studies of Canadian history inevitable. The familiar turns out, on examination, to be foreign, or almost so—related, recognizable, but not perfectly comprehensible using the prism of American experience, politics, or institutions. A first theme of Canadian history, accordingly, is that of a distinctive political culture.

The major distinction that strikes travelers through Canada is size. Size need not mean geography. Canada is a vast land, but so is the United States. And Americans can travel to more, much more, of their own country than Canadians can to theirs. Much of Canada is largely inaccessible and much more of the country is uninhabitable.

The Canada that Canadians know is, in fact, much smaller than the United States, although strung out for more than 3,500 miles in a long band north of the U.S. border. In that 200-250 mile band live roughly 26 million Canadians, approximately one-tenth the population of the United States. This proportion is a useful one to keep in mind. It has been relatively constant throughout most of Canada's history and is a serviceable piece of background information. By itself it helps to explain much of Canada's economic and foreign policy and some of Canada's internal politics.

Although Canadians readily accept the fact that their population is smaller than that of the United States, they would be surprised and perhaps pained to learn that their population is also somewhat less than that of Poland, Romania, or Spain. Thus Canada's size, especially in relation to the United States, is a second and inescapable theme in the country's history.

Canada's population is not only small but subdivided. Most Canadians speak English and therefore count as English Canadians or "anglophones"; the "anglo" tends to refer to language rather than ethnicity. But some 26 or 27 percent of Canadians speak French; in the past century the number of French speakers has hovered around the 30 percent mark. The language frontier runs, on the east, through the province of New Brunswick, and on the west along the Ottawa valley, roughly between Ontario and Quebec. Significant pockets of anglophones live in Quebec and of francophones in Ontario, New Brunswick and Manitoba. Although locations and proportions have changed somewhat, this distribution has obtained for over a hundred years. The division between English and French Canadians is one of the first that must be grasped in dealing with Canada; in the words of Hugh MacLennan, a well-known Canadian novelist, Canada's two principal language groups live in "two solitudes." These linguistic solitudes are a third strand in Canada's history.

There are jurisdictional divisions as well. Like the United States, Canada was endowed with a federal government, located in Ottawa. Also like the United States, Canada has regional governments, called "provinces." In 1867, when the Dominion of Canada was constituted, there were four provinces; since 1949 there have been ten provinces and two territories. As in the United States, there are and have usually been conflicts between regional authorities and the central government. The intensity of such conflicts has varied greatly over time, but whether they are called provincial or regional, they form a fourth abiding theme in Canadian history.

All these themes were present when, in 1867, three scattered British colonies (Nova Scotia, New Brunswick, and "Canada") were united into what was called the Dominion of Canada by a statute of the British Parliament, the British North America Act. Canadians called the process *confederation*, a term that can give rise to some confusion, for what was established was more like a *federation*, with a genuine central government. The Dominion of Canada was still a British colony, a larger and more powerful colony than its predecessors or its constituent parts, but still firmly British territory. The facts that the British Parliament could rearrange Canada's boundaries, legislate its political constitution, and even regulate its civil establishment showed what colonial status meant for Canada.

The British found it unprofitable as well as unwise to attempt to control the details of governing a colony such as Canada. The American Revolution served as a lasting example of the possible consequences of such a policy. The British Parliament did not, therefore, try to raise revenue in Canada; Canadians taxed themselves or not, as they pleased. By the same token, the British spent little in Canada and were trying to reduce what little they did.

2

Defense was the crux of Canada's relations with Britain in the 1860s. Only one country could conceivably conquer Canada: the United States. Defense against the Americans appeared to the British government to be an increasingly unreasonable proposition. It would soak up a large proportion of the British army and navy at a time when they might be needed in India, the Far East, or the Mediterranean. Furthermore, despite occasional panics (in 1861-62, or 1864, during the American Civil War), it did not really seem that the Americans wished to go to war over Canada.

If relations with the United States could be peacefully regulated, Canada would virtually disappear from Britain's list of external anxieties. If the Canadians had quarrels of their own with the United States, the British made it increasingly plain that they did not wish to be involved. The Canadians protested, but they proved unwilling to carry their complaints to the point of severing their connection with Britain. And so the Canadians remained British. Although their spokesmen wrote of a "new nationality," they meant a new *British* nationality, for to be British was, among other things, to be separate, to be different, from the United States.

For most Canadians in 1867, being British was a positive value. Instead of having a president, Canada had a queen, Queen Victoria. Queen Victoria was not an especially outstanding intellect or personality, but such was the strength of her position that she gave a tone, as well as her name, to most of the nineteenth century: the Victorian Age. The queen, as the British and Canadians knew very well, reigned but did not rule. Her ministers were chosen from among the majority in the British Parliament, and some of them she disliked intensely. But that mattered little to her adoring subjects, and as her reign grew longer (it lasted from 1837 to 1901), she became more and more popular.

In Canada, which she never visited, her portrait hung on schoolroom walls, in post offices, and in family parlors. She personified British prestige; perhaps she even magnified it. It was just as well, for the British government overrode majority opinion in Nova Scotia and manipulated politics in New Brunswick to secure the entry of both provinces into confederation. As for Quebec, its reward was that it was divorced from its preconfederation twin, Ontario. The old Province of Canada was divided, creating a Francophone majority in Quebec and an Anglophone Ontario. Quebec's limited autonomy was pronounced to be satisfactory, especially by French Canadians; given the limited nature of midnineteenth century government and the existence of a powerful federal government in Ottawa, it did not seem that the Anglophone minority had much at risk. They had, in any case, a guarantee of separate Protestant schools in Quebec; in reciprocity, Catholic schools in Ontario also were guaranteed. English and French became official languages in the federal Parliament and in the Quebec legislature. The guarantees reposed in the British North America Act; it would take an act of the British Parliament to change them.

As a colony, Canada was not sovereign, Britain was. The British government conducted foreign policy, made treaties, and declared war. A British cabinet minister, the colonial secretary, handled relations with Canada. His local representative, the governor general of Canada, was a British aristocrat, usually with political connections, enough, at any rate, to qualify for what was considered to be a prestigious but undemanding post. The governor general might influence government, but he did not run it. That was the business of elected Canadian politicians, who occupied themselves with raising revenue, dispensing patronage, and defining internal policy. Only in the broadest sense was the governor general part of "the government."

The government belonged to whoever could command a majority in the lower house of the Canadian Parliament (the House of Commons), or, as the case might be, in the provincial legislatures. At first glance, these institutions closely resembled their American counterparts across the boundary line. They were popularly elected and based on locality. As in the United States, there were national political parties that extended their grasp into the furthest reaches of municipal politics (or occasionally vice versa). There was (and is) a Senate, whose members were re appointed for life; there were equal numbers of senators from each major region of Canada. The Senate was comparable to the British House of Lords; it had the power to reject any legislation it chose, but because it was appointed rather than elected, it seldom flexed its legislative muscles. In an all-out confrontation with the elected House of Commons, it was assumed that the Senate would lose. It had the power, therefore, to delay, obstruct, and annoy, but it was not a politically significant body. Nevertheless, a senatorship was highly prized, and senators were, after 1867, appointed by the prime minister from among his supporters.

Unlike the United States, the executive branch in Canada has long since formally surrendered to the legislative branch. Party leaders combined executive function with legislative leadership, and they were expected to prove themselves daily in parliamentary combat with their political foes. Canada, like Britain, had a prime minister and a cabinet whose members were almost all, and almost always, elected and electable. The prime minister was the head of the largest parliamentary grouping, or party.

Canadians took their politics very seriously. There were two general political tendencies in 1867. The government party was a coalition of interests cobbled

4

together by Canada's first prime minister, Sir John A. Macdonald. He called it the Liberal-Conservative party, but almost everyone soon called it simply Conservative or Tory. Confronting Macdonald were the Reformers or Liberals; their nickname was (and still is) Grits (for determination). Such was the power of partisanship that, within a very few years, politics in the provinces and throughout the nation was organized on Conservative and Liberal lines; the party chieftains sat in Parliament at Ottawa.

There were resemblances to the American party system, especially as expressed in Congress in the nineteenth century. As in the United States, politics was cemented by patronage, and patronage implied rigid devotion to the party and its interests. The prime minister, as party leader, was the fount of reward, whether the reward was a contract, a job in the post office, or a judgeship. The provincial premiers were equally sovereign in their own spheres. Such a system placed a premium on loyalty and conformity; rebellion against a leader became an increasingly grave matter. It took a while for the system to be fully implanted, but by the 1880s strict party votes were the norm.

In 1867, Ottawa, a lumber town situated on the Ottawa River that divided the provinces of Ontario and Quebec, became the capital of the new dominion. It had formerly been the capital of the province of Canada. Ottawa had the makings of a handsome city, with four largish rivers, a couple of waterfalls, and a canal; its Parliament buildings were pleasant and impressive, if not exactly distinguished.

But Ottawa was not the largest, or even the wealthiest city in Canada. That was Montreal, a hundred miles down the Ottawa, where that river flows into the St. Lawrence. Montreal was a river port, and more: it was the head of deep-water navigation on the St. Lawrence and therefore a major transshipment point to the railroads and shallow canals that served the interior. It was also a banking center, and an industrial city. In the 1860s, it was predominantly English-speaking, but its factories were attracting numbers of workers from the surrounding countryside. The countryside was mostly French, and in the 1870s the balance in the city tipped; Montreal became predominantly French-speaking, although still with a large Anglophone population. As a rule, the language of banking and of management generally was English. French Canadians wishing to carve out a business career—and there were prominent and wealthy French Canadian capitalists—understood that they would make their way in a predominantly English-speaking milieu.

Montrealers, both English- and French-speaking, looked down on the only city that aspired to rival them: Toronto. Toronto was the capital of Ontario, a lake port, railway center, and manufacturing town on Lake Ontario. Toronto also had its banks, which were increasingly successful after 1867. Unlike Montreal, it was ethnically homogeneous, English-speaking, and overwhelmingly Protestant; also unlike Montreal, it could draw on a larger agricultural hinterland, for which it acted as a wholesale distribution center.

The other large cities (the term is relative) included London and Hamilton in Ontario, and Quebec City, the capital of the province of Quebec. But Canada thought of itself as rural rather than urban; of the country's 3.5 million people, no more than 20 percent lived in cities, towns, and villages.

The maritime provinces, Nova Scotia and New Brunswick, had several regional metropolises: St. John on the Bay of Fundy, and Halifax, the Nova Scotian capital. Both were much smaller than Montreal or Toronto; although neither was economically insignificant, they were not well placed to dominate the trade and commerce that flowed to and from their inland rivals. The two provinces had prospered in the age of wooden ships and sail, but that age was obviously drawing to a close and maritimers were not sure what would replace it. They had some options—lumber and coal—but the population was too small to sustain large-scale industry, and it was inconveniently scattered. There was not even a railroad link to the interior; although one was promised as part of the arrangements of 1867, it took ten years to build. Anxiety bred suspicion, and as the maritimes failed to grow in the years after 1867, a sense of grievance arose. Thanks to a rigid party system, that resentment did not always find expression, but occasionally it broke forth.

The limited nature of nineteenth-century government has already been noted. Governments taxed little and spent, usually, less. The Canadian government had impressive powers, in theory: over trade and tariffs, transport, most courts and criminal justice, defense and external relations, and immigration, to mention only a few. The provinces, in contrast, controlled what were thought to be pre-eminently local matters: municipalities, roads, courthouses, education, and property and civil rights. Residual power, over subjects not mentioned in the original division of powers, belonged to the federal government. The intention was to avoid giving too much power to the provinces; after all, it was believed, the Americans had just had to fight a civil war because too much power had been given to the states. And so the Canadian constitution was constructed in response to the American one; yet its later history would be very different, as will become evident.

As originally constituted, Canada was a long, narrow ribbon of land that stretched from the height of land between Lake Superior and Hudson Bay to the Atlantic Ocean and did not include all the British territory in North America.

On east coast there were two colonies that did not join Canada in 1868. Prince Edward Island, a small agricultural colony perched off the coast of New Brunswick, had experienced a railroad boom followed by a financial bust. Despite a brief flirtation with the Americans, Prince Edward Island had virtually no choice but to seek financial relief through joining Canada, which it did in 1873.

Newfoundland, larger, farther away, and less closely linked to the mainland, was another matter. Newfoundlanders faced outward, to the Atlantic and the fishery; their markets were not in Canada, but in Europe or the West Indies; and both the colonial, mercantile, elite in the capital, St. John's, and the Irish-dominated Catholic church were, for various reasons, strongly opposed to joining Canada. And Newfoundland did not join (although the question recurred in the 1890s, in the 1910s, and in the 1930s) until 1949.

The West and the North presented other issues. The vast region drained by Hudson Bay, including virtually all of what is now the Canadian prairie, fell under the jurisdiction of a British company, the Hudson's Bay Company . The company found itself unequal to the task of running its vast domain. Its goal was to make profits, but it could not reconcile profit taking with the expensive and increasingly heavy burden of government. American settlement was pushing toward the frontier; existing settlements, especially at Red River (present-day Winnipeg), were unruly; and the fur trade, the company's principal business, was increasingly confined to remoter areas. When Canada approached the company with an eye to purchase, the company was happy to unload its increasingly troublesome heritage in return for cash and a substantial grant of land—real estate that it hoped to sell to settlers at a considerable profit.

The transfer was to take place on 1 December 1869, and Sir John A. Macdonald duly dispatched a governor to take possession. The inhabitants of Red River, however, had other ideas. Under the leadership of Louis Riel, a Metis (Metis are of mixed European and Indian descent), the Red River colony rose in rebellion. They demanded guarantees of political rights and land tenure, and forced the Canadian government to concede them. Red River accordingly became Manitoba province and existing land titles were guaranteed. Unfortunately, there had been some bloody incidents and although Riel's demands were granted, Riel himself became an outlaw, fleeing before the arrival of British and Canadian troops in August 1870. Instead of a constructive force, Riel became a negative symbol of resistance, disappointed hopes, and western alienation from eastern domination. Not everyone subscribed to those symbols, but the Catholic and largely French-speaking Metis felt increasingly uncomfortable in Manitoba as white settlers moved in from Protestant, English-speaking Ontario. Many of them accordingly moved west, to the valley of the Saskatchewan River, in hopes of better times; Manitoba, which was bilingual at its foundation, became an English-speaking province. Indeed, because the French Canadians took little interest in distant prairie settlement, English became the dominant language throughout the West.

In the short run, the objectives of the Canadian government were achieved. It absorbed the lands of the Hudson's Bay Company between the forty-ninth parallel and the Arctic Ocean. Ten years later, in 1880, the British government donated the Arctic islands as well (not all of them were know; as late as the 1920s new islands were being discovered and added to the Canadian landmass). Canada occupied the prairies and opened the land for settlement. And, having reached the Rockies, it could beckon to the one remaining British colony in North America, British Columbia.

British Columbia was a relatively recent settlement, with a white population of 12,000. Its politicians agreed to join Canada in 1871, if Canada agreed to build a transcontinental railroad to link the eastern provinces with the Pacific; Macdonald agreed.

Why not? The country was prosperous, its trade flourishing, its rulers optimistic. But a transcontinental railroad was a tall order, and it challenged Macdonald's skills to put together a syndicate that could raise the necessary capital to build one. The prime minister was not choosy about his instrument, and his negotiations with businessmen happened to coincide with a hard-fought federal election in 1872. Macdonald needed, and got, campaign contributions, and the syndicate got a federal charter to build a railroad. Even for the pragmatic political morality of the nineteenth century this was too much; a political scandal—the Pacific Scandal—resulted. Macdonald's supporters deserted him. He lost his majority in the House of Commons and resigned. A new election in 1874 ratified the result: the Conservatives were out, and the Liberals, under Alexander Mackenzie, were in.

Macdonald had been a smooth and supple leader, an able lawyer, and a natural compromiser. Mackenzie, originally a stonemason, was none of these things. Although he had ability, he was not a gifted leader; rather, he was obsessed with a sense of personal responsibility, a sentiment that had not troubled his predecessor. His cabinet contained some gifted ministers, particularly Edward Blake from Ontario and Wilfrid Laurier from Quebec, but it was better noted for its quarrels and disagreements than for its policies.

Mackenzie's record was not barren. Operating in an unfavorable economic climate (trade was off and government revenues were down), he nevertheless tried to build the Canadian Pacific Railway in bits and pieces. He established a Canadian Supreme Court. He tried to restore integrity to the central administration. He also became deeply unpopular, and in 1878 the Liberals were turned out of office as Canadians returned to the banner of the charismatic Macdonald.

In the 1878 election Macdonald promised to raise tariffs to protect Canadian industry. This doctrine was, of course, directed largely against American imports, but Macdonald and his followers hoped to persuade American businessmen to establish themselves in Canada, thereby strengthening the Canadian economy, giving Canada and its government the sinews of nationhood. Appropriately, Macdonald's high tariffs (enacted in 1879 and thereafter) were called the National Policy. It worked, after a fashion. It did not create boundless prosperity, but it undeniably favored industry and it established an industrial clientele, capitalists and labor, that depended on tariff protection for its continued existence. Ever since, industrial ambition and economic nationalism have been important forces in Canadian politics and life.

Using the National Policy and identifying it with western settlement and improvements in transportation, Macdonald defeated the Liberals again in 1882. The Conservatives in that election proved to be popular in all parts of the country, although the difference in seats in the House of Commons was somewhat greater than the actual spread in the popular vote. But it was the last election for some time in which Ontario and Quebec voted the same way.

The year 1884 was a bad one on the prairies. Western settlers, white and Metis, were unable to obtain satisfaction from the federal government. To attract Macdonald's notice, they sought out a proven attention-getter, Louis Riel, then living in the United States after a brief spell in an insane asylum. Riel was only too pleased to leave Montana and return to Canada by popular demand. Unfortunately, Riel was not the man he once had been.

Once ensconced among the Metis of central Saskatchewan, Riel gave way to grandiose religious fantasies, featuring himself as a major prophet. Early in 1885, rebellion broke out. There was considerably more bloodshed than in 1870, and in less time. Whereas in 1870 it had taken months to transport troops to the West, in 1885 it was a matter of a few weeks. Macdonald had finally succeeded in encouraging a syndicate that could build a Canadian Pacific Railway, and in 1885 the railway was within months of completion; enough existed to move troops and supplies swiftly to the West.

Riel and his followers were defeated at Batoche, the last battle fought on Canadian soil. Riel was arrested and tried for treason. Riel denied his own defense, which turned on the issue of his insanity, and he was duly condemned to death. Despite an outcry from Quebec, where the French-speaking Riel had become a national symbol, the federal cabinet approved his execution.

Dead, Riel became a martyr in Quebec. The Conservative party took the consequences, both provincially and federally. In the 1887 election, Macdonald's support in Quebec shrank; in the next election, 1891, the Liberals took the lead in that province. They have since retained it in every election but two, with notable consequences for Canada's political system.

Riel was not the only factor in the Conservative decline among French-speaking Canadians: poor leadership, scandals, and factionalism took their toll. But Riel set matters in motion; it only remained for the Liberals to take advantage of the opportunity thus presented.

For a time the Liberals failed to do so. The ineffective Mackenzie was disposed of in a coup in 1880, but his successor, Edward Blake, was no better at attracting popular support. After losing the 1887 election, Blake gave way to his Quebec colleague, Wilfrid Laurier.

The choice of Laurier was, for its time, rather daring. He was a French-speaking Catholic in a predominantly English-speaking, Protestant country. Linguistic and religious differences were taken very seriously indeed in a society where religion was a basic organizing principle. Foxe's *Book of Martyrs*, chronicling the gory history of the Reformation, was standard fare in Protestant households, whereas Catholic clergy strove to preserve their flock from the harm done by excessive liberalism and secularism. Religious quarrels were not simply a French affair; Protestant and Catholic Irishmen brought their differences to Canada and battled in the streets on festive days. In Ontario, a provincial election in the 1880s turned on the religious implications of an item on the school curriculum.

Nor were English-speaking and French-speaking Catholics to be found on the same side. Control of church property and appointments was a lively issue at the end of the nineteenth century. Like Protestant-Catholic mistrust, it lingered into the twentieth.

Laurier was, as might be imagined, exceptionally sensitive to questions of race and religion. (Language issues in this period were usually called "race questions.") Fluently bilingual, Laurier was also personally lukewarm in matters of religion. With no strong convictions of his own at stake, he was prepared to seek out compromise. It might even be said that he erected compromise into a political panacea. Believing strongly in personal liberty and freedom of choice, Laurier argued that there need be no clash between religion and liberal politics; in his form of liberalism, religion was a matter for private conscience and choice. The state should, at most, facilitate that choice, not dictate it.

Race and religion, although important, were not the sole issues preoccupying the electorate. Prosperity and the economy counted as well. Economic controversy centered on the tariff, and the tariff issue was usually focused on relations with the United States. Between 1854 and 1866, British North America, as it then was, and the United States had reciprocally abolished certain tariffs. The Americans terminated this tariff regime, called reciprocity, in 1866, but many Canadians wanted it back. Macdonald, as part of a British delegation sent to Washington, tried his hand at negotiating reciprocity in 1871. The British had a range of issues to negotiate, and in the end all that Macdonald achieved was a favorable, if temporary, resolution of fishing rights off the Atlantic coast. There would be no reciprocity because the Americans were not interested.

The Liberals tried in 1874, with no better success. The Conservatives, when they returned to power in 1878, remained disposed to reciprocity, but the American attitude was always the same: no. Reciprocity in some form nevertheless continued to attract some Canadian voters, especially farmers, who resented the high cost of Canadian-made manufactured goods. Laurier sought to turn this sentiment to political advantage by proposing for the 1891 federal election "unrestricted reciprocity" or "commercial union."

It should have been plausible. Canada was not thought to be abounding in prosperity. Canadians perceived that their American cousins were paying cheaper prices for commodities, and that the United States offered greater employment opportunities. If emigration is substracted from immigration for Canada's first four decades (that is, 1861-71, 1871-81, 1881-91, 1891-1901), the result if a figure called net immigration, and it is a negative number. That is, more people left Canada in the last four decades of the nineteenth century than arrived there. Some of these were immigrants who had started overseas and were simply moving on, but many more were native Canadians. According to the 1900 U.S. census, there were 1,179,922 native Canadians living in the United States, a figure equal to 22 percent of the contemporary Canadian population. Only a high birthrate allowed Canada to grow at all. By 1901 the term *American cousin* had literal and quite common meaning.

The meaning applied to French as well as English Canadians. During the years after Confederation, farmers drifted to the cities, as a result, Montreal changed from predominantly English-speaking to French-speaking. But French-language migrants did not stop at the border. They continued south, to the industrial cities around Boston, and they stayed. Over time, they lost their language and most of their distinctive culture, but the fact that they were going to a foreign melting pot did not inhibit their departure. Some no doubt took comfort in the fact that New England was closer to Quebec than the Canadian prairie, and some may have cherished the illusion that New England, or parts of it, would become French-speaking. In retrospect, it is obvious that outside the sheltered political environment of Canada, where the French language was recognized and institutionalized, even proximity would not defend it. Politics and language appear, from this vantage point, to be inseparable. So volatile was the mixture that the temptation to keep politics restricted to other, less dangerous, topics was overwhelming. For Laurier, economics, a subject that he had not especially studied, must have seemed a blessed relief.

Laurier's economic policy had its attractions, but not enough. Against the Liberals, Sir John A. Macdonald revived the cry of simple patriotism. The National Policy was a guarantee of Canada's difference from the United States, as symbolized by the British Empire's Union Jack. Under the banner of "The Old Man, the Old Flag, the Old Party," Macdonald triumphed in March 1891. Exhausted by the campaign, he died three months later.

The Conservatives were still, of course, in power, but they had no luck with their successors to Macdonald. The first, the aged Sir John Abbott, lasted less than a year. The second, Sir John Thompson, a Nova Scotian, was vigorous, active, and intelligent, but he died at the end of 1894. The third, Sir Mackenzie Bowell, was elderly and unintelligent; he is generally considered Canada's least competent prime minister. He lasted for rather more than a year, until dissension in his own party, accompanied by the feeling that under Bowell the Conservatives were doomed to lose the next election, brought about his downfall. It was by then 1896. With the Conservative mandate expiring, (Canadian Parliaments are elected for five-year terms), a general election was scheduled for June.

The next prime minister, Sir Charles Tupper, was a powerful politician, but he had too little time to consolidate his position before the election, and his party was crippled by controversy over sectarian (Catholic) schools in Manitoba. Tupper tried to sustain Manitoba's Catholic minority against the homogenizing policies of the provincial (Liberal) government. But in Quebec, where the Catholic church mobilized its forces behind the Conservatives, the bishops discovered that the electorate were most attracted by the fact that the Liberal leader, Wilfrid Laurier, was a French Canadian. That Laurier refused to take a firm position on Catholic schools in the West bothered the Catholic voters not a whit.

With Quebec behind him and Ontario evenly divided, Laurier won. Twenty years younger than Tupper (he was fifty-five), he ended a period of geriatric politics dominated by figures who had grown up when Queen Victoria was young. Laurier, many hoped, would be a man of the twentieth century.

## Liberalism and Imperialism, 1896-1921

During the late nineteenth century, foreign affairs impinged very little on Canada. Canada was part of the British Empire, and the empire was at peace—at peace, that is, with any country that could seriously challenge Britain. During the 1870s, 1880s, and 1890s the empire was expanding, sometimes peacefully, sometimes not, but never in the face of resistance from any great power. Britain's empire was vast, the British navy the world's largest, and the British economy the most prosperous. Few indeed were the countries where there was no British investment, for the British were exporting their economic surpluses to Russia, to South America, and to North America.

Canada was happy to take investment wherever it could find it. Prior to 1900 that meant mostly British investment; after 1900, in terms of direct investment, that meant mostly American. Because Canadian language and law were already quite familiar to British and American capitalists, no great strain was involved. Much of the money went wherever the capitalist judged best, but some of it went where the government intended, which, in the years after 1900, meant mostly railroads.

Between 1895 and 1915, Canada's railroad system expanded rapidly, from 16,000 miles of track to 46,000. Two new transcontinental railroads were laid down, the Canadian Northern and the Grand Trunk Pacific. Both involved government assistance in varying degrees, for the very good reason that the railroad companies could not easily see how they were to make an adequate profit. As it turned out, they could not make a profit at all. The great railroad adventure ended in a government investigation, nationalization, and in the 1921s, the creation of a vast government-owned railroad system, stretching from the Atlantic to the Pacific, called the Canadian National Railway. It competed directly with its older rival, the Canadian Pacific Railway, from head offices a few blocks apart in downtown Montreal, which continued through this period to be Canada's transportation hub.

The railroad net was both a cause and a consequence of one of the most important developments in Canadian economic history, the Great Wheat Boom of 1896-1914. Briefly, the terms of trade for Canadian exports turned strongly in Canada's favor during the 1890s. Shipping costs fell, export prices rose, and new technology made primary production cheaper and, in some cases, made it feasible.

Most regions of Canada shared in the economic upturn, but it was most spectacular on the prairies. One measure of economic advance is the population a region can support. In 1901 the Canadian prairies had a population of roughly 420,000; in 1911 it was 1,330,000; and 1921 it was approaching 2 million. Immigration went up, too; from 16,835 in 1896 it rose to 272,409 in 1907; then, after a slight dip, it went up again, reaching 400,870 in 1913, the highest figure ever. The foreign-born population of Canada rose from 699,500 in 1901 to 1,955,725 in 1921; the largest single component among the foreign-born, however, was from the British Isles—more than 1 million of the 1921 total. (The next-largest group, 374,000 in 1921, was from the United States.)

The wheat-growing lands of the West were parceled out among the settlers. Because new and hardier strains of wheat had been developed, farming could go farther north than anyone had previously imagined, to the Peace River country in northern Alberta and British Columbia. Because the rains were good, settlement in the dry belt, called Palliser's Triangle after its first surveyor, seemed to be feasible. Because the federal government, in 1897, negotiated a deal with the Canadian Pacific Railway, freight rates for transporting grain were lower than they otherwise would have been, and this, too, encouraged western settlement.

The organization of western settlement was the responsibility of the federal government. Even in Manitoba, Ottawa had retained control over crown (government) land and mineral rights. The rest of the prairies were organized as the Northwest Territories. As in the United States, territories passed through a system of direct rule, with a government appointed from Ottawa, and then through a period of shared responsibility between elected local representatives and federal civil servants.

Politically, the prairies were managed by Laurier's powerful minister of the interior, Clifford Sifton; Sifton successfully recruited immigrants from eastern and central Europe as well as the more traditional British sources. When the immigrants reached Canada, they were strongly attracted to Laurier and Sifton's Liberal party, a development that proved to be a second stage in the Liberals' development. Besides being identified with French Quebec and Catholics outside that province, the Liberals increasingly became the party of recent immigrants. Although immigrants were not their sole source of support, they were

14

significant. Sifton also managed to identify the Liberals, for the time being, as the party of the West and the wheat farmer; but that identification later brought about difficulties.

In 1905, the prairies were judged to be ready for provincial status. There was no particular difficulty about dividing the territories into three parts. The North remained under direct federal jurisdiction, and the South was cut into two provinces, Alberta and Saskatchewan. As in Manitoba, the federal government retained control of crown lands and minerals. An attempt by Laurier to regulate the school system provoked a crisis in his cabinet; although the crisis was resolved, it showed the volatility of relations among Canada's principal religious and racial groups. As it turned out, Alberta and Saskatchewan were closer to the Manitoba model of development. Ethnically, half the population derived from the British Isles, either directly or several generations back, and they set the political tone.

As a rule, Laurier preferred to leave such issues as schools to local option. Both in opposition and in government, Laurier sang the praises of provincial rights, and during his time in office he rebuffed attempts to attract the federal government into provincial spheres. He well remembered that in the 1870s and 1880s Sir John A. Macdonald had fought endless, and largely fruitless, jurisdictional battles with the provinces. Those battles had come back to haunt the Conservatives in the 1896 election, and Laurier was not eager to see them repeated.

When the Conservative government of Ontario took steps to take over (on behalf of the province) electrical power generation and transmission, Laurier refused to come to the aid of aggrieved British investors. If Ontarians wanted to turn on provincially generated energy, he would not hinder them or attempt to extend federal jurisdiction.

Although Laurier's time in office coincided with the Progressive Era in American history, the Canadian party system withstood the onslaught of regulated virtue somewhat better than its American counterpart. Many of the same issues popped up. In Ontario, as has been shown, the issue of public ownership was resolved against "the interests" and in favor of a broader definition of public involvement. The definition, however, drew its support from manufacturers and local entrepreneurs who believed they would receive fairer treatment through the political system than they would through the operations of an unregulated market.

As in the United States, civil service reform became an issue, and it was resolved in much the same way. Conservation reared its head and was adopted as a cause by Clifford Sifton. And, like the American Midwest, the Canadian prairies discovered a sense of grievance against the eastern economic interests that dominated federal economic policy and plundered western consumers through the tariff.

Laurier attempted to respond to the West by concluding a reciprocity agreement with the Republican Taft administration in 1911. He then allowed himself to be maneuvered into an election by the Conservative opposition in Parliament, and when the smoke cleared, he had lost. Reciprocity in 1911, as in 1891, raised the possibility that Canada would surrender one of the most vital parts of its identity, its ability to set its own economic policy. That a third of the country—especially the West—thought that policy damaging and mistaken had to be set against the fact that two-thirds of Canadians, especially in Ontario, approved of the existing tariff structure.

But had the 1911 election been on tariffs alone, Laurier might not have lost it. Unluckily for him and the Liberals, it was about much more. To understand this conundrum, it is important to go back fifteen years.

Laurier was not free to conduct Canadian-American relations in a vacuum. Canada was still part of the British Empire, and after 1896 the empire increasingly demanded attention. Although still impressive, prosperous and powerful, Britain had been losing ground economically to the United States and to Germany. British relations with the United States were on the whole placid, but British relations with Germany and with the whole of continental Europe were fragile.

How fragile, a crisis in 1899 demonstrated. In far-away South Africa, the British Empire had come into conflict with two Dutch-speaking settler states, the Orange Free State and the Transvaal. The Afrikaners, or Boers, as they called themselves, invaded British territory in October 1899 and, in the months that followed, defeated everything the British sent against them.

To its consternation, the British government found scant sympathy abroad for its predicament. Britain had no allies, and it soon appeared that it had no friends either. Only its colonies rallied to the cause and sent troops. But in Canada's case they were not sent without a political crisis.

Laurier knew that the British government was eager to find ways of persuading its more prosperous and mature colonies to support its policies. The colonial secretary, Joseph Chamberlain, had said as much at a conference of colonial prime ministers in London in 1897. Laurier also knew that his English-speaking fellow citizens might well find the imperial idea—or imperialism—attractive. French Canadians, however, did not. They preferred to be left alone. They were happy to be a protected minority within the empire, but they did not want to send

16

their children on English-speaking crusades in support of causes they did not understand. In Henri Bourassa, a young member of Parliament, this attitude found a powerful spokesman.

In the autumn of 1899 the two Canadian attitudes, English-speaking imperialism and French-speaking isolationism, met and clashed. Laurier eventually worked out a compromise that allowed Canadian volunteer units to go to South Africa on the understanding that the British would pay for them when they got there. The compromise was accepted. The troops went, fought in several battles—the British were winning by the time they arrived—and returned home covered in imperial glory. French Canadians did not object to volunteers' getting themselves killed in foreign wars; nor did they object to the modest expenditures on horses and saddles and uniforms (many of them made in Quebec) that the war entailed. In the November 1900 general election, Laurier swept Quebec and most of the rest of the country too.

The South African war ended in 1902. That year, an imperial conference of the self-governing British colonies was held in London; it was conveniently timed to coincide with the coronation of the new British king, Edward VII, which every self-respecting colonial with sufficient influence wished to attend. There was another appeal for a systematic contribution to British defense from the colonies, which Laurier sidestepped ("that damned French dancing-master," one delegate growled).

Even if Laurier had agreed to more Canadian involvement in British foreign and defense policies, he would have had difficulty in defining what those policies should be. The British faced eastward, toward Europe; Canada's government was concerned mostly with its own backyard in North America, and therefore with the United States.

There was a dispute over the Alaskan boundary, which had achieved importance with the discovery of gold in the Yukon in 1896. The gold rush of 1897-98 followed, and so did police and administrators and, of course, customs officers. The boundary had been defined by a treaty of 1825 between Britain and Russia, which had then owned Alaska. The question was whether the boundary followed the general line of the coast, which would have put some key inlets in Canada, or every twist and turn of a very indented shore as the Americans contended. The American contention was probably the stronger one, and the Canadians were rash to reject several early attempts at compromise. Finally, a judicial tribunal was set up, consisting of three Americans, two Canadians, the British lord chief justice, and in 1903 it rendered its decision. On almost every issue it ruled for the Americans, by a vote of four to two.

The difficulty was not so much the details of the decision, as the manner by which it was arrived at. President Theodore Roosevelt had let it be known that he would accept no decision unfavorable to the United States, and the American arbitrators he appointed were strong partisans of his point of view. (To be fair, the Canadian arbitrators were no better, but they lost.) Canadians present at the arbitration had no doubt that the British had simply decided that American friendship was too important to be sacrificed for Canada, and that in any case there was nothing that could be done to alter Roosevelt's position. So, they reported, Canada had been sacrificed instead.

There can be little doubt that from the British point of view the decision was the right one. Britain did not want, and certainly did not need, a quarrel with the United States. The Alaskan boundary question was not a specially important issue, even for Canada; doubtless the Canadians would get over it. So they did, but not without some serious geopolitical reflections and, for some, the conclusion that although the British Empire was only too happy to have Canadians defend it, such a defense was a one-way street.

The Alaskan boundary dispute pointed up the necessity for Canada to improve its relations with the United States. The British embassy in Washington, which handled Canadian-U.S. relations, wanted Ottawa's dealings with Washington to be put on a more regular, reliable, basis; messages sent to Ottawa often got lost because there was nobody there to answer them. Under British pressure, Laurier established a Department of External Affairs in 1909 to run the files and make sure that correspondence received an answer. Intended as a housekeeping bureau, External Affairs nevertheless became a center of knowledge and interest on foreign-policy—the first such in Canada. At the time, the Canadian and U.S. governments agreed in 1909 to regulate transborder disputes over water and pollution and similar matters through an International Joint Commission. Like the Alaskan boundary tribunal, it had three members each; unlike that body, it tried to render its decisions on the facts of each case presented, and it was relatively successful.

It was in the context of generally good and improving Canadian-U.S. relations that Laurier made his reciprocity agreement of 1911. The rest of the international horizon was, however, not so cheery.

Sensing its relative economic decline and knowing that it could not hope to defend its far-flung empire on its own, Britain sought out allies. It found, first, the Japanese in 1902, then the French in 1905, and finally, in 1907, the Russians. Their common rival was Germany, which threatened British control of the seas. To melt this threat, the British engaged in a naval race, building as many battleships as they could afford. To afford more, they turned to their colonies for assistance.

This request for help presented Laurier with the same dilemma he had faced during the South African war. British Canadians would wish to help the British, French Canadians would not. Laurier's compromise this time was an autonomous Canadian navy that would be placed under British control in time of war. The conservative opposition derided it as a "tin-pot navy" and demanded that Canada instead pay for a couple of battleships that could directly join the British Grand Fleet in European waters. Henri Bourassa denounced Laurier's naval policy as far too pro-British.

In the election of 1911, Bourassa and his French Canadian nationalists joined forces with the imperialist Conservatives in defeating what they both disliked, Laurier. The fact that they agreed on nothing else they left for the future, and a new prime minister, to take care of.

The new prime minister, Sir Robert Borden, was a dour, though not untalented, Nova Scotian, but the naval question defied his talents. As a result of the fundamental divisions on the matter between Conservatives and Liberals, and between English and French Canadians, Canada still had no naval policy, and hardly any navy, when war broke out in Europe in August 1914.

Public opinion and politicians of all stripes responded to the British cause. The Germans had invaded neutral Belgium and violated international law; they were threatening Britain; they were on the point of defeating France and Russia. Canadian volunteers rushed to the colors, and within a few months the first of hundreds of thousands of them were on their way across the Atlantic to join the British Expeditionary Force in France.

Only Henri Bourassa asked why, and even he waited a couple of months to speak out. At first he had little impact, but as the war dragged on, as war hysteria in English Canada grew, and as casualties mounted in France and Belgium, his point of view was increasingly noticed. Laurier took note. He did not underestimate the force of Bourassa's appeal in French Canada, and he was well aware that French Canadians were, for a variety of reasons, increasingly exasperated with their English compatriots. He knew that Borden was ineffective and unconvincing in French Canada. Ontario had chosen just this moment—with the support of the Irish Catholic bishops—to prohibit French-language schools in the province, and attempts to sway the Conservative government of Ontario to reconsider proved spectacularly fruitless.

When, in 1917, Borden decided that only conscription would produce enough reinforcements for the Canadian army in Europe, he provoked a political crisis of the first magnitude. French Canadians were opposed, most English Canadians were in favor. English-speaking Liberals joined the Borden government to help speed conscription through; French-speaking Liberals (and some others) stuck by Laurier. In an election in December 1917, Canada was split very nearly on racial lines. Laurier was left to lead a mostly French-speaking Liberal opposition party in Parliament.

It should be emphasized that Laurier and French Canada were still acting within the Canadian political system. It was the Liberal party that sat in Parliament, not a French Canadian nationalist party. Bitter alienated though they might be, French Canadians had not abandoned Canada. This was in some ways Laurier's greatest achievement, but it was also his last, for he died shortly afterward, in February 1919.

The conscription crisis was not the only crisis to afflict Canadian society during World War I. The Canadian economy was mobilized to support the war. There was full employment and round-the-clock munitions production. At first, the war production was bought by the British, but by 1917 the British were running out of cash. To pay for the rest of the war, the Canadian government sought loans in the United States and raised hundreds of millions of dollars through "Victory Loan" drives. After the United States entered the war in 1917, the American government cooperated with Canada in war finance and war production, thus affording some relief to the hard-pressed Canadians. Financially, at least, Britain was giving way to the United States as a source of external funding, a further sign of Britain's weakening position in the world.

The Borden government's economic policies unintentionally stimulated rampant inflation in Canada. The price of everything shot up. Even though workers were paid more than ever before, they were still losing ground. Union organization and strikes were the result. Those who blamed the economic system for their woes found solace in the Bolshevik revolution of 1917 in Russia; in 1918 and 1919 they could be sure of at least sympathetic hearing in union halls across Canada.

When the war ended with Germany's defeat in November 1918, it was none too soon. Canadian society was politically, racially, and economically polarized. That Canada had held together under the strain was a sign of inherent strength, but Canadian leaders were certain that they never wanted to experience such a combination of crises again.

Sir Robert Borden believed that Canada's contribution of troops, supplies, and money to the empire's war effort had won his country the right to be consulted, and heeded, in the formulation of British foreign policy. The British had established consultative mechanisms, including an Imperial War Cabinet, where empire leaders could meet together privately and arrive at effective decisions, and some of the decisions they made were important. Borden hoped that this could continue. At an imperial conference in 1917 he persuaded his empire colleagues to pass a resolution in favor of a better-structured empire. In such an empire, the senior self-governing colonies—the Dominions—would have equal status with the British government. Thus, although Borden certainly counts as a Canadian nationalist, he was also a British imperial nationalist. Canada would, he believed, make its voice count in world affairs in combination with its British partners.

At the Paris Peace Conference that concluded the war, Borden had British support for autonomous Canadian participation, both in the conference and in the League of Nations that it established. But Borden intended to use Canada's status in an empire sense, and at Paris he was a loyal participant in the British Empire delegation. He hoped that this policy could continue, and he believed that the conference experience was a good sign.

It was not a foolish thought, but once the pressure of war was removed, all the components of the empire, including Britain, tended to revert to their prewar patterns of behavior. The British wanted Canadian support, but they did not need Canadian advice. At an imperial conference in 1921 this attitude was made plain, to the discomfiture of the Canadian delegation under Borden's successor, Arthur Meighen. It was left to Meighen's successor, Mackenzie King, to draw an appropriate conclusion.

The war had been too much for Borden and his government. Borden collapsed in September 1919, and, although his colleagues persuaded him to take a rest cure, he never again fully functioned as prime minister. He resigned in 1920 and was succeeded as head of a Conservative-Liberal coalition by Meighen.

Meighen had been an effective government spokesman in the past. He was instrumental in implementing conscription, he had helped shape the nationalization of the bankrupt railroads, and he had helped crush a general strike in Winnipeg in 1919. He was controversial, and he did not shy away from disputation. A believer in a high protective tariff, he had scant sympathy for farmers' complaints about the National Policy. As an honest man, he made a point of telling them so.

In retrospect, it was not surprising that Meighen lost the election of 1921. His government carried the burden of all the most unpopular measures of the war. He could do nothing about farmers' demands for a lower tariff and a more favorable economic system.

The man to whom Meighen lost was, ironically, a former college classmate. William Lyon Mackenzie King had been a minister under Laurier, a labor expert for the Rockefeller interests in the United States, and a Laurier Liberal in the 1917 election. He had the support of Quebec and of the traditional Liberal vote in eastern Canada. He, too, could do nothing much about farmers' discontent, but he did not go out of his way to confront them. Mackenzie King saw Canadians as divided into two basic categories: Liberal voters and potential Liberal voters. The former were to be stroked, and the latter encouraged. To such a personality, Meighen was the obvious foil.

The election of King and the Liberals in December 1921 put an end to a decade of confrontation. King was determined that Canada should never again have to endure such a test.

## Isolationism and Depression, 1921-1939

Canada, an Alberta member of Parliament remarked in 1921, had had enough in the way of foreign affairs. It was time to concentrate on Canada.

This was not an unreasonable conclusion, given the tensions that war and its aftermath had brought. Foreign affairs were disturbed element in Canadian life, and it was high time to minimize them. As prime minister, Mackenzie King placed a premium on "national unity" and identified war as the prime disruptive force in Canadian politics. Every four years, at election time, Liberal party orators in Quebec reminded Quebec voters of conscription, thereby putting the recent and painful memory of disunity in the service of King's version of unity. Most French Canadians wanted no more foreign adventures, and many English Canadians agreed with them. But not, as King knew, the majority. The empire still stood, Canada was a member, and, war or no war, most English Canadians considered themselves to be British.

King understood their feelings, and up to a point he shared them. As he told an imperial conference in 1923, if a "great and clear call of duty" ever came, Canada would be at Britain's side. There is no evidence that the British took King's assurance seriously; in 1939, when King actually carried out his promise, the British government was mildly surprised, and grateful.

The British should not have been surprised. King knew that most Canadians did not want to get involved in minor imperial skirmishes abroad. When war threatened between Britain and Turkey in 1922, King stood aside. When Britain involved itself in guarantees of European frontiers in the 1920s, King sent best wishes but no commitments. He would not let his country's support be taken for granted, nor would he permit foreign policy to become the subject of routine debate in Canada. Any such debate would not be routine, because it would raise fundamental differences between English and French Canadians. If there had to be a debate, King preferred that it be on an issue of life or death. To help him understand just when life and death were at stake, King increased the strength of his Department of External Affairs and recruited a small but brilliant cadre of professional foreign service officers. Henceforth there would be at least some independent Canadian reporting on trends in international affairs. Some of the officers, needless to say, were disappointed to learn that what King required of them was analysis, not action.

What action there was was symbolic. During the 1920s the Dominions succeeded in defining their status as autonomous and effectively independent countries, united to Britain only through a common language and a restricted number of common institutions, including the monarchy, and, of course, the monarch (George V through most of the interwar period). Canada therefore acquired the right to send ambassadors abroad, and the colonial secretary's jurisdiction over Canada finally lapsed.

And so Canada between the two world wars adopted a minimalist foreign policy. Canada was a member of the League of Nations and played a constructive, though minor, role in its deliberations. A small group of Canadians, including King's French Canadian political lieutenant, Ernest Lapointe, took a benevolent interest in the League as an instrument for peace. Lapointe's interest and support for the League did not extend to trying to make it a decisive force in international relations. When crisis arose before the League, Lapointe preferred to disengage, and so did Mackinzie King, in the best interest of pragmatism and democracy. King liked to use the phrase, "Parliament will decide"; until then, there would be no policy.

Disengagement was a major feature of the King governments in the 1920s. The federal government had become hyperactive, in King's opinion, and very expensive. A fiscal conservative, King preferred to reduce programs (such as unemployment offices), avoid new commitments (such as health insurance), and reduce the national debt. He had the best of reasons, he told Parliament. Social policy belonged to the provinces. By reducing the national debt and by gradually lowering federal taxes, he was making room for those Canadian governments that actually had the constitutional responsibility for health and welfare.

That argument could only take King so far. In the mid-1920s, opinion in the maritime provinces focused on the fact that their economies were in a continuous slump. Political action was demanded, and, after a lively agitation and a learned investigation, some relief was given in the form of subsidies and other concessions. The idea dawned that not all provinces could afford an acceptable level of social services, because their economies, and therefore their tax base, were insufficient to support what people had come to expect.

Federal and provincial support programs were one solution; emigration, whether to other parts of Canada or to the United States, was another. Canadians migrated towards provinces with higher per capita incomes and higher rates of employment; that meant that they moved away from the maritime provinces, away from the countryside, and into cities. The 1921 census was the last one that showed a majority of Canadians living in rural areas. And although many moved into town, many others chose to leave the country altogether. During the 1921-1931 decade, 1.2 million persons immigrated to Canada, but 900,000 Canadians left, mostly for the United States.

As the standard of living rose and leisure time increased, Canadians, like Americans and western Europeans, demanded more of their institutions, that is to say, of their governments. For example, school years lengthened and students got more of them until, in 1931, Canadian students spent an average of ten years in school and left at age 16. Students in the maritimes and in Quebec left earlier, and those in the prairies stayed longer. Secondary schools increased in number, grew larger, and acquired more facilities—"frills," according to the cost-conscious. The number of university students increased, as did the proportion of women at university, reflecting changes in the larger society. Nevertheless, the higher the degree of education, the fewer the women; Ph.D.s were an almost exclusively male preserve.

Schools, roads, and hospitals help to explain why provincial governments and cities were spending more in the 1920s and why the proportion of provincial expenditures, compared with those at the federal level, was increasing. That being so, it is not surprising to find that during the 1920s the provincial governments became assertive, if not actually aggressive, in pressing demands for more revenue and more jurisdiction. Their record of success is impressive. The prairie provinces secured control over their natural resources and public lands; the maritimes, as was already mentioned, received more subsidies; and Quebec and Ontario acquired limited federal jurisdiction over waterpower. Together, the provinces successfully limited the federal government's ability to amend the constitution, an achievement that some of them later came to regret. The British Parliament in 1931 conceded that it could no longer make laws for Canada, but it still had the duty of amending the Canadian constitution whenever Ottawa and the provinces could agree to ask it to do so. That painful duty remained intact until 1982, the last vestige of Canada's colonial past.

The augmentation of provincial activities during the 1920s did not worry Mackenzie King. He was busy reestablishing the Liberal party in areas where it was weak, such as among farmers, and in frustrating the talented Arthur Meighen and the Conservatives. King came within a whisker of losing the 1925 federal election, but was saved, for a time, by the support of farmer members of Parliament (the so-called Progressives). King lost his majority in Parliament when a customs scandal broke in 1926, and he resigned at the insistence of the governor general, Lord Byng. He soon rebounded, defeated in Parliament a minority government headed by Meighen and then won a general election in the fall of 1926. Meighen departed and so did Lord Byng, the undeserving target of King's political scorn.

King had by then practically absorbed the Progressives, leaving only a radical rump outside the Liberal fold. With Quebec solid behind the Liberal party provincially and federally, the odds favoring Liberal victory increased dramatically, but not, as will become evident, conclusively.

King proved unequal to coping with the Great Depression, which began in 1929-30. The slump in Canada was exacerbated by overcapacity in certain industries, such as pulp and paper, and by the swift collapse of certain commodity prices, such as wheat. To compound the misery, the mid-1930s saw a dust-bowl on the prairies, as the rains failed and Palliser's Triangle returned to its naturally arid state. Unemployment rose, welfare rolls increased, and some provinces began to beg for money to meet the demands being placed on them. King's response was unimaginative, not to say uncharitable. He would not, he told Parliament, give "a five-cent piece" to a Tory provincial government for the purpose. The Conservative opposition, led this time by R. B. Bennett, a Calgary corporation lawyer, was quick to exploit the opportunity afforded by the Depression and defeated King in the 1930 general election.

Bennett was in his own way as unimaginative as King. King had no policy that could cope with economic slumps; Bennett did, but his preferred solution was to raise Canadian tariff. This measure was only to bargain with others, he told the electorate: fair trade rather than free trade. He would then "blast a way into the markets of the world." He did not, but he did raise the tariff, in tandem with the Americans and many other countries. Tariff walls around the world did not help to cure the Depression, as economists had predicted. But economists were not much listened to or regarded.

Bennett, like King, believed in local autonomy, but he did not have the luxury to put his belief into practice. Most of Canada's nine provinces soon reached the limits of their ability to tax or borrow enough funds to feed the welfare system. Bennett could not let them go bankrupt, because that would damage the country's credit rating and imperil the national finances. So, grudgingly and gracelessly, Bennett forked out cash to the supplicant provinces; and they reciprocated by biting the federal hand that fed them. By 1935 every province but one boasted a Liberal government; the exception, Alberta, elected a radical populist party, Social Credit, that promised to print money out of thin air.

Fortunately, Social Credit's monetary system was outside provincial jurisdiction. When the Alberta government tried to legislate some of its milder programs, the efforts were firmly squelched by the federal government and the courts. The federal government by then was back in Mackenzie King's hands. A last-minute attempt by R.B. Bennett to cloak his government in New Deal clothing, reminiscent of the Roosevelt administration across the border, failed. All Bennett succeeded in doing was to unsettle his own Conservative voters, many of whom turned to Mackenzie King, whose slogan, "King or Chaos," had a real effect in the 1935 federal election.

The Canadian people got King, but they were no closer to ridding themselves of the Depression. Perhaps that did not matter so much as some have believed, for the 1930s proved to be a remarkably conservative decade in terms of politics and policy. Conditions in 1935 and 1936 were markedly better than they had been in 1932 or 1933, the depth of the Depression. Nevertheless, gross national product remained low; it would not reach 1929 levels again until 1940.

It was apparent to the majority of Canadians that the causes of the Depression were vast and probably unmanageable by any domestic agency. The weakness of provincial finance was obvious, especially when compared with the relative strength of the federal government. And so, outside Quebec, the 1930s were marked by a drift towards centralization. English Canadians, and even some French Canadians, looked toward Ottawa for solution; some provincial governments were more than willing to divest themselves of their jurisdiction over welfare and social policy if it bought them relief from the crushing costs of unemployment and poverty.

Even in Quebec there was political movement. In 1936 the Liberal provincial government that had lasted for thirty-nine years was defeated and replaced by a National Union government made up of provincial Conservatives and dissident Liberals. Its tone was more nationalist and traditionalist than reformist, however, and its main accomplishment was a lavish spending program.

26

Mackenzie King had no solutions to offer. In the late 1930s he was at his wit's end to find policies to combat the Depression. What he feared most was pressure to spend money, but he was overtaken by events. Europe was rearming; Britain was rearming. The Nazi regime in Germany seemed bent on war, and, reluctantly, King nerved himself to propose a modest rearmament program to Parliament. Lapointe and French Canadian opinion moved with the prime minister, step by slow step. King had never been in doubt that if Britain and Germany went to war, Canada would have to join in. He was aided by the rapacity and rapidity of Hitler's aggressive policy. Even isolationist Canadians were shaken by events in Europe; and they were appeased by the frantic attempts of the British government to avoid war. If war came, it would not be Britain's fault. Finally, in March 1939, King and Lapointe told Parliament and the world that if war came, Canada would be in it. Canada's British alliance was honored; but King and Lapointe had so managed events that the two linguistic groups did not come to blows, or to open division, on the issue. As in 1914 and 1917, the Canadian political system withstood the shock.

It would not be a war like the one in 1914, Lapointe promised Quebec. There would be no conscription. Lapointe was only partly right. It would not be a war like the 1914-18 one.

## Prosperity and Growth, 1939-1957

When Canada entered World War II in 1939, many observers believed that racial conflict and social disruption of the kind Canada had endured between 1917 and 1919 would deal the Canadian political system a blow that might prove fatal for nationhood. This dark prophecy proved inaccurate. There were some general reasons why this was so. The war was fought far from Canada's shores, and Canada suffered almost no physical damage from the conflict. Because of the course of events overseas and the caution of British generals under whom Canadians fought, Canada had fewer casualties in the longer war than in World War I. Advances in the understanding of administration and economics enabled Canada's western provincial governments to cope rather better with the demands of war than their predecessors in 1914 had done.

There were also factors that were peculiar to Canada. The Liberal party was, in 1939, in an extremely strong political position. Its leader had elevated compromise and obfuscation to an art form, and his talents were entirely appropriate to the management of apparent opposites. He dominated his cabinet without offending many of its members, and his cabinet was of exceptionally high caliber. He called a snap election in March 1940, promised no conscription, and overwhelmed the opposition. Enfeebled, the opposition Conservatives and Canada's nascent socialist party, the Cooperative Commonwealth Federation (CCF), were unable to mount any serious political challenge to the Liberals during the war.

The cabinet presided over a bureaucracy that was well educated, experienced, and small enough to achieve a genuine unity of purpose and practice, as well as esprit de corps. It taxed and borrowed and controlled wages and prices in proportions that avoided the horrendous inflation of World War I; prices in 1945 were actually below the levels that had prevailed at the end of the previous war. The government managed labor conflict in a generally enlightened way. Although some strikes occurred, there were never as many as in 1917 or 1918. Politicians and bureaucrats together strove to avoid profiteering and scandals (there had been quite a few between 1914 and 1918), and even in that delicate category they usually succeeded.

To raise necessary revenues, the federal government had to rationalize Canada's often confused tax system. With taxes rising to pay for the war, the federal government decided that it must occupy all important tax fields (income, succession, and corporation taxes). It arranged in 1941 to "rent" these fields from the provinces, paying each province an agreed rental that would cover its costs. The provinces had little choice but to agree.

Canadian industry had to bear an unusually heavy load during the war. Fortunately, some industries had not fared badly during the Depression. The large automobile manufacturing sector could be converted to producing trucks. Locomotive shops were, with less success, converted to tank production. An aircraft industry was created from the ground up. Almost all tools had to be imported, not to mention plans and management skills; some came from Britain and some from the United States. But almost all the war executives were home-grown. Canadian-made planes rolled from the factory to the training fields, where Canada hosted a huge British Commonwealth (as the empire was by then called) Air Training Program.

Paying for production and training was not easy. National income r see harply during the war. Victory loans and taxation raised substantial sums, but exports were crucial. Britain could not help; it was effectively "broke," as the British ambassador in Washington put it. Only the United States had the money. Luckily for Canada, U.S. war production lagged about a year behind Canada's, so Canada had products to sell that the Americans needed. Through the Hyde Park

28

agreement of 1941, the U.S. and Canadian governments created a single system for purchases of war supplies. Although not quite free trade, it immensely simplified cross-border transfers.

It was the business of the politicians, as well as of the bureaucrats, to raise the necessary manpower to staff industry as well as the armed forces. This was no easy task, and for some years it defeated the efforts of statisticians trying to estimate how many workers, skilled and unskilled, there actually were, and where. Industry fought with the military for scarce labor, but it cannot be said that either side definitively won the battle. What seems to be certain is that there were simply too few workers and soldiers for all the work that had to be done, especially in 1943-44.

Labor scarcity and a shortage of military manpower eventually produced the same crisis that had occurred in World War I, but the King government was better prepared than Borden's had been. When the Allied armies in Europe were routed by the Germans in the Spring of 1940, and France fell to the enemy, King and Lapointe had steered conscription for home defense through Parliament, with almost no resistance inside or outside Parliament. Lapointe's death was a setback, but a new recruit to the cabinet, Louis St. Laurent, took his place as French Canadian lieutenant. Then, in the aftermath of Pearl Harbor, King pushed through a referendum that asked voters whether they would release the government from its pledge of no conscription for overseas service. The electorate, with most of Quebec opposed, said yes. St. Laurent supported King, and conscription, in the referendum.

In 1942 it was only conscription in theory. In 1944, with casualties mounting in Normandy and Belgium, it became conscription in fact. St. Laurent again supported King, who, until the last minute, positively refused to send anyone but volunteers to Europe. But at the end of 1944, conscripts, including many French Canadians, were sent and they were needed.

The Canadian government avoided an active foreign policy between 1939 and 1945. Although Canada was, relatively speaking, a much more important Ally (the fourth largest, militarily and in war production) than it had been in World War I, Canada's military contribution was a long way behind that of Britain, and still further behind those of the United States or the Soviet Union. Mackenzie King played host to two major conferences between Winston Churchill and Franklin D. Roosevelt but after the publicity photos were taken, he retired from the scene.

It might be thought that King's sinuous political style would fail to attract votes in the aftermath of his broken promise not to send unwilling troops abroad, but fortune favored King and the Liberals. The war in Europe ended in May 1945. Although Canada was involved in the war against Japan, its Pacific role was minor. Only a small number of soldiers were expected to be sent to join in the invasion of Japan. Soon the troops would be coming home, and even before that the electorate was called to pronounce judgment on the Liberal's record and on their promises for the future.

The election of June 1945 turned on the question of security: social security as well as the international variety. The government had presided over full employment; it presented an attractive package of veterans' benefits; and it had a moderately progressive record on such things as labor policy. Most important of all, with the war over, conscription was just not an important issue in Quebec. In a year when the general trend of opinion was toward the left, the Liberals offered just the right mixture of progressivism and demonstrated managerial capacity. Narrowly, they won the election.

The Canadian government faced three major policy questions: What kind of international system could Canada help to achieve? What kind of domestic society did the Canadian government wish to legislate? What should the balance be between federal power and provincial responsibility in postwar Canada? The answer to each question bore on the other two.

If, for example, the postwar world was assumed to be hostile and uncooperative, it followed that wartime controls should remain in place and that defense expenditures should remain relatively high. If prosperity turned on central planning and if the lessons of the 1930s were to be properly applied, federal power must prevail over provincial rights. If security of individual income was foremost, the same conclusion must follow. But if prosperity was hampered by regimentation, federal predominance was less desirable or appropriate.

The Canadian government was unable to contemplate a world organized around confrontation. Six years of war were enough; indefinite mobilization of manpower and resources was too much. Public opinion demanded that the government bring the troops home, and home they came, and back into civilian life.

Civilian life was well able to absorb them. Unemployment barely rose at the end of the war, and soon settled back to a comfortably invisible level. The government busied itself reducing taxes; but because it was simultaneously launching a number of social programs (a children's allowance was the most notable), expenditure on nonessentials was cut to the bone. One nonessential was the country's armed forces, which were qreatly reduced. Their number rose again a few year later, but even twenty years after World War II, Canada's peacetime soldiers were eking out the last of their wartime materials.

Canada's senior civil servants and most of Mackenzie King's senior ministers believed that their wartime record qualified them to prescribe a dose of Liberal economic planning for the country. At federal-provincial conferences in 1945-46 they urged the provincial governments to concede social policy, including health insurance, to the federal government. Unemployment insurance had already been surrendered to Ottawa in 1940, and old-age pensions had been shared since the 1920s by both levels of government. By adding in health insurance and a few other items, Canada could achieve a comprehensive social support program that would be the same in all regions of the country. This would relieve the less-prosperous provinces, such as the maritimes, of the burden of justifying less-adequate programs to their electorates.

Canada's richest provincial government, in Ontario, did not see the matter that way. Arguing the case for provincial rights and local autonomy, Ontario effectively blocked a national, comprehensive, social security system. It also demanded its taxation rights back and, in 1947, it got them. Quebec, which, after an interlude of Liberal rule from 1939 to 1944, was back under the control of the conservative National Union party, took the same stand. Its premier, Maurice Duplessis, preferred that his province keep its own distinctive institutions, not be subject to homogenization at the hands of an English-speaking majority.

The clock was not turned back to 1939, but it did not race ahead as some of Ottawa's planners and politicians would have liked. Nevertheless, their hopes were not entirely in vain. Their ambitious social security proposals of 1945 set the Canadian political agenda for the next twenty-five years; in one way or another, all their ideas—comprehensive pensions, hospital insurance, and health insurance generally—were eventually enacted. And, in 1952, Ontario reentered the national tax system. Canada kept its national unemployment insurance program, although there was slight need for it in the prosperous years after 1946. In 1951, old-age pensions were, by a constitutional amendment, declared to be entirely a federal responsibility. Hospital insurance followed in 1957, but as a joint federal-provincial program. Meanwhile the federal government churned out budgets conceived according to the best Keynesian countercyclical principles; thanks to the general prosperity of the time, these budgets were generally in surplus.

Why was Canada prosperous? Planners in 1945 expected that prosperity would derive from trade, but statistics show that this was not the case. In the years after 1945, exports did not rise but imports did. In most years, from 1950 on, Canada ran a current account deficit. The difference was made up by capital imports, mostly American. These imports were welcomed, by government as broadening Canada's industrial base, by ordinary citizens as affording new products, and by labor as providing jobs. Some critics deplored the proportion of American investment and lamented the dominance of American companies, methods, and values in Canada. But although from time to time these lamentations struck a nationalist chord, they lacked any consistent, across-the-board impact. Even in years when Canadians were politically annoyed with Americans, they continued to believe that what the Americans had to offer, whether in automobiles, advertising, or management strategies, was better than any conceivable alternative. The 1950s, and the 1960s too, were thus very American decades.

The prosperity was accompanied by a rise in the standard of living, second only to that in the United States. Canadians, like Americans, bought cars, stoves, refrigerators, and houses in the suburbs. A federally funded mortgage corporation encouraged private homeownership and, except in Quebec, the majority of homes were by 1961 owner-occupied. Television arrived via American border stations and, in 1952, via the Canadian Broadcasting Corporation, the government-owned network.

Broadcasting was only one example of a mixed economy, mostly private but partly public, in which government owned an odd mixture of things including an airline, a river barge company, a uranium mine, a nuclear engineering firm, and a hydroelectric network. Capital expenditures were mostly provincial in the years immediately after World War II, but in 1951 the federal government again took the lead. There was a war in Korea and thus a need for rearmament.

The hopes the Canadian government had placed in the international system proved to have been exaggerated. Canada maintained important contacts with its two principal wartime allies, the United States and Britain, but after the discovery of a Soviet spy ring in Ottawa in 1945, Mackenzie King was reluctantly prepared to draw pessimistic conclusions about Soviet intentions.

By the time King retired, in 1948, Canada was negotiating the shape of the North Atlantic Treaty with the Americans and British and in 1949 Canada became a founding member of NATO. King's successor as prime minister, Louis St. Laurent, was much more inclined to take a proportionate share in the common defense. When the Korean War broke out in 1950, Canada sent ships, planes, and eventually an army brigade to fight under the United Nations banner. In 1951, alarmed at the possibility that Korea might prove a prelude to Soviet aggression elsewhere, the Canadian government dispatched a brigade group and an air division to Europe.

These Canadian actions expressed St. Laurent's conviction that solidarity with the liberal democratic societies of Western Europe was an essential component in Canada's foreign policy. Although Canada, like every other Western country, relied on American nuclear weapons to deter Soviet aggression, Canadians also believed that a small country's conventional military forces helped make a difference in the strategic balance between East and West. In addition, Canadians saw their military effort as expressing an identity of political purpose between the two sides of the Atlantic Ocean. Lester B. Pearson, the external affairs minister, expressed the hope that NATO would eventually prove to be more than a military alliance—that it would discover economic and political functions as well.

This concept termed "Atlanticism" for lack of a better name, held an exaggerated importance for Canada because of the simultaneous and continuous decline of British power. In the years after World War II, the Canadian government did its best to bail out the British with loans and credits, but Canadian aid by itself was hardly enough to help. Although Canada attempted to be an active and supportive member of the British Commonwealth, it could not avoid noticing, slowly, that the Asian and African ex-colonies of Britain did not closely resemble the British model from which they sprang. The Commonwealth became, at best, a useful talk-shop and a means of exerting informal influence. It was no substitute for the British Empire.

In the absence of such a substitute, the United States assumed disproportionate importance in Canadian life. Canadians were aware that the United States was their most important trading partner, investor, and military ally, and most of the time they were grateful for the American presence. But they worried that the presence was overwhelming and that Canada's distinctive identity, forced to stand on its own, without British support, at a population ratio of ten to one, might be swamped.

St. Laurent and the Liberals bore the brunt of this national uneasiness. They had won large majorities in the House of Commons in elections in 1949 and 1953, but after 1953 their luck ran out. They lost their touch in Parliament and came to appear arrogant and aloof. The cabinet was aging; half its members were old-age pensioners. In 1957, St. Laurent called an election that he expected to win easily only to discover that his election machine had grown rusty. He found that Canadians believed that his government was too close to the United States and too far from Britain. He learned that American investment, even if it contributed to Canadian prosperity, was regarded as a mixed blessing. And on election night, 10 June 1957, he was surprised to learn that the Liberals had lost the election.

The election of 1957 was perceived as a turning point in Canadian history. It turned out the Liberals, the governing party, and replaced them with the Progressive Conservatives, the latest name for Macdonald's old Liberal-Conservative party. It rejected a party based on Quebec, as the Liberals had been, and substituted a party that derived much, if not most, of its strength from Ontario. Conservative partisans later claimed that it tried to replace the rule of the senior civil service, "the mandarins," with a populist government based on the rule of the people. The new prime minister, John Diefenbaker, who had never run anything larger than a prairie law office, was meant to exemplify this change.

In fact, things changed very little. The Diefenbaker government, which originally held a mere plurality of seats in the House of Commons, swiftly called another election that trounced the Liberals and equipped the government with a massive majority. Yet Diefenbaker embarked on few bold initiatives. He did nothing to stem off the flow of foreign (mostly U.S.) investment into Canada. He swiftly established a warm relationship with the American president, Dwight Eisenhower, who, like Diefenbaker, was a prairie boy born in the 1890s. Diefenbaker had no background and little information that allowed him or his ministers to contradict the civil servants when they offered advice. As a result, Diefenbaker's time in office, 1957 to 1963, was an era of civil service dominance tempered by political expediency. Diefenbaker, having won office after twenty years in opposition, was terrified of losing it. Although Diefenbaker had a flamboyant personality, his government was politically timid. Appearance, under Diefenbaker, was so often at variance with reality that even when the prime minister offered good news to his electors, it was not believed.

One piece of good news that he might have confided to them was that the economy was in fundamentally good shape. The rate of growth diminished between 1957 and 1959, but growth there was; and in 1961 Canada embarked on another economic boom. Unluckily for Diefenbaker, the boom was accompanied by a higher unemployment rate than Canadians had been accustomed to in the postwar period, and so the economic good news was not believed.

Although he did not realize it at first, Diefenbaker symbolized another message. The great prosperity of the 1950s had not been all-inclusive. It was less in the maritimes than elsewhere, and less in certain parts of the prairies. The Canadian government could not compete with the American government in subsidizing wheat sales, and as wheat shortages and high prices were replaced by a wheat glut, prairie farmers blamed the Ottawa government for their inability to

34

sell their product. Diefenbaker, however, came to office just as China discovered a drastic shortage of grain and as the Soviet Union experienced a series of disastrous harvests. The good civil servants of the Canadian Wheat Board, which managed Canada's wheat marketing, discovered their opportunity. The politicians, including Diefenbaker, took the credit, and the considerable popularity that accrued. Although the prairies had favored the Liberals ever since the days of Laurier and Sifton, they did not do so any longer. As Quebec moved toward support of the Liberals after 1957, Manitoba, Saskatchewan, and Alberta leaned toward the Conservatives. As Diefenbaker's credit declined in the rest of the country, it soared in the prairie provinces. Regional political differences thereby took on a new dimension just as French Canadian "nationalism" was undergoing one of its periodic rebirths.

Quebec nationalism had always appealed to a segment of French Canadians. Under the premiership of Maurice Duplessis (1936-39 and 1944-59) it was channeled in a conservative direction. As the federal government attempted to venture further and further into income support and educational subsidies, the government of Quebec returned a firm negative. By 1960, the Quebec middle class was ready to turn in another direction, and that year the Liberal party under Jean Lesage was elected. Lesage presided over what was called the Quiet Revolution, during which the provincial government expanded into social services; the size and competence of the provincial bureaucracy substantially increased; and, inevitably, a contest developed with Ottawa for funding. Lesage, essentially a moderate, seemed unable to control the liberal nationalists in his cabinet, who took heart from the nationalization of roughly half the province's hydroelectric firms in 1962. (The first half had been nationalized back in 1944, under a previous Liberal government.) Henceforth the language of work in this important industry would be French, not English.

Diefenbaker was unable to respond to, or even to understand, the increasing agitation in Quebec over matters of language and jurisdiction. The opposition Liberals, under Lester B. Pearson, proposed a commission to investigate "bilingualism and biculturalism" in Canada, and although Pearson was not spectacularly successful in picking up Quebec seats, he got enough there and elsewhere in the 1962 federal election to place Diefenbaker in a minority position.

That was crucial for Diefenbaker, who was caught in an unwinnable quarrel with the new American president, John F. Kennedy. He resented Kennedy's youth and style, and he believed that Kennedy preferred the more internationally minded and cosmopolitan Pearson (who had won the Novel peace prize in 1957). Diefenbaker was unable to make up his mind over the stationing of U.S. nuclear warheads in Canada, and he was similarly unable to offer support to Kennedy during the Cuban missile crisis of 1962. When Diefenbaker publicly pretended that relations with the U.S. were better than they actually were, Washington issued a denial. This pushed the tottering Diefenbaker government close to collapse and Diefenbaker's tactical political errors did the rest. Three ministers resigned, Diefenbaker lost a vote of confidence in the House of Commons, and after the general election of April 1963, the Liberal party formed a minority government.

Pearson promised "sixty days of decision," an ill-chosen phrase that tempted the embittered Diefenbaker and his forces to discredit the new government. Thanks to Pearson's minority position and the Liberals' tactical ineptitude, Diefenbaker succeeded in reducing the House of Commons to a shambles during the two parliaments of 1963-65 and 1965-68. Nevertheless, the Liberals managed to introduce a revamped, universal pension plan (the Canada Pension Plan), universal health insurance, a unified armed force, and a new flag. Abounding prosperity and a gradual reduction in the defense budget helped to pay for it.

At the same time an apparently endless succession of scandals, Liberal and Conservative, was paraded into public view. The effect was to weaken the prestige of the federal government at a time when it was enacting one of Canada's most ambitious legislative agendas. The beneficiaries were not the opposition parties (Progressive Conservatives, the New Democratic Party—the CCF's successor—and Social Credit) but the provincial governments. Pearson therefore faced not merely fractious opposition in Ottawa but belligerent provincial administrations that resented having to reorder their priorities in order to accommodate Ottawa's new social programs.

Pearson had been a successful external affairs minister between 1948 and 1957, when, in the aftermath of World War II and its devastation, Canada had played an active and relatively prestigious role abroad. But since Pearson had left office in 1957, Europe and Japan had recovered from the war, and although Canada remained prosperous, its relative standing as a world power sank. The United Nations, in which Canadians placed great hope during the 1950s, failed to develop into a powerful or impartial international arbiter. The outbreak of the 1967 Arab-Israeli war and the simultaneous expulsion of a Canadian peacekeeping force from Egypt further reduced the United Nations' prestige and undermined the credibility and popularity of Pearson's foreign policy. Pearson had his hands full with the unpopularity of U.S. involvement in Vietnam. Although Canada was not a belligerent in that war, Canadian public opinion mirrored the divisions of U.S. opinion on the subject. For a government that founded its international policy on alliance with the United States, this was an extremely uncomfortable time. Pearson managed to offend both the U.S. government and some vocal segments of Canadian public opinion by appearing to take both sides of the Vietnam issue.

In short, the Pearson government by 1967 had run its course and exhausted its credit. An intervention by French President de Gaulle in 1967 ("Vive le Quebec libre!") revealed deep divisions between opinion in Quebec and opinion in the rest of Canada; for the first time, there was a possibility that Quebec nationalism and the assertiveness of the Quebec government would lead to that province's withdrawal from Canada. In December 1967, Pearson announced that he would retire the following spring; it helped that Diefenbaker's party had already retired its unwilling leader.

Pearson's successor was a first-term member of Parliament, his justice minister, Pierre Elliott Trudeau, a Montreal writer and professor. The selection of Trudeau as Liberal leader in 1968 was a measure of his own off-beat attractiveness, but it also indicated how very worried the Liberals were about Quebec. Trudeau, Liberals guessed, would be decisive and effective in handling Quebec and they were right.

Trudeau, a stylish forty-eight-year-old bachelor, became the object of the phenomenon of "Trudeaumania." He swept the country in the 1968 federal election and although, as a Liberal, he did not carry the prairies, he did better there than any other Liberal since 1953. Given a majority in the June 1968 federal election, he used it to reduce Canada's foreign commitments, especially to NATO (half the Canadian troops in Europe were brought home); to address the question of reforming the Canadian constitution; and to secure its "patriation," an unusual word that in the Canadian context meant acquiring the power to amend the constitution entirely within Canada, without having to rely on a vote of the British Parliament. Trudeau also stimulated the greater use of French in the essentially English-speaking Ottawa bureaucracy, and promoted strong and competent French-speaking ministers to give "French power" in the national capital a higher profile.

In October 1970, confronted by an outbreak of separatist terrorism in Quebec, Trudeau called in the army, suspended civil liberties in that province, and discouraged any attempts at compromise with the terrorists. Although many people objected that his use of power was disproportionate (some five hundred persons were arrested), terrorism, which had been on the rise in Quebec, sharply declined. At the same time Trudeau's intervention did little to quash legal, non terrorist separatism. Indeed, in 1976 the separatists, under Rene Levesque, triumphed in a provincial election and formed a government.

Trudeau's attractiveness to English-speaking voters declined over time, although in federal elections he maintained his hold over many voters in Quebec who were simultaneously casting ballots for Levesque. In the 1972 federal election, Trudeau barely won a plurality in the House of Commons, and for the next two years he clung to power with the help of the semisocialist New Democratic party. During those two years the federal government showed a tendency to spend more money more freely; it also established a Foreign Investment Review Agency to respond to the concerns of those Canadians who wished to restrict the expansion of American investment. A federal oil and gas company, Petro Canada, was formed.

When an international oil price rise of unprecedented scope occurred in 1973-74, the federal government acted to control prices in Canada. It used tax on Canadian oil exports to subsidize the price of petroleum in the maritimes and Quebec, which were dependent on high-priced imports from overseas. The West complained that, having paid for the Canadian tariff for a hundred years, the least it deserved was the ability to charge other Canadians market prices for its non-renewable products. Trudeau, however, was able to arrange a compromise with the government of Alberta, and the crisis in the West never quite came to a boil. Nevertheless, it did little to make the Liberals more popular on the prairies, and rumblings of prairie separatism could from time to time be heard.

In 1974, however, Trudeau's charisma and astute political maneuvering allowed him to defeat the opposition in a federal election and to control a majority of seats. But Canadians appeared to find his performance disappointing, and certainly the next five years were not distinguished by any spectacular triumphs at home or abroad.

In 1979 a minority Progressive Conservative government under Joe Clark was elected. Clark was unlucky. After the elegant Trudeau, the new prime minister looked like a bumbler. He promised conciliation between the federal government and the provinces—notably lacking under Trudeau—but, failed to deliver. He was unable to satisfy aggressive Conservative governments in Alberta and Newfoundland, and he lost the confidence of the Conservative government of Ontario. Clark was described in a popular joke as suffering from "amsirahc"—the reverse of charisma. After miscounting his probable support in a crucial vote, Clark was defeated in the House of Commons and swept away in the subsequent federal election of February 1980. "Well, welcome to the 1980s," Trudeau told a national television audience.

Trudeau returned just in time to deal with Rene Levesque and his separatists. Levesque had scheduled a referendum in Quebec to equip himself with a popular mandate to negotiate "sovereignty-association" for Quebec: political sovereignty, but an economic association with the rest of Canada to allay anxieties that Quebec would suffer economically from its departure from Canada. The federalist forces were ostensibly led from within the province, but their real inspiration was Trudeau, and Trudeau prevailed on referendum night, 20 May 1980. The separatists suffered a crushing defeat, winning only 40 percent of the vote; even if only French Canadian votes had been counted, the separatists would have lost. Trudeau, not Levesque, had a mandate from the voters of Quebec.

But what mandate? In May 1980, Trudeau promised Quebecers "renewed federalism." The effect of that promise is unclear. What Trudeau made it, the federalist forces were already virtually certain to win, and so it is unlikely that his words by themselves motivated very many voters to switch their votes. And in fact what Trudeau did was to set the constitutional machinery in motion, and fast. "Allons-y Cadillac," one of his member of Parliament quipped: Let's go in style, a Cadillac, to whatever destination Trudeau chooses.

The revision of the constitution would prove to be Trudeau's crowning achievement, but at the time it was one event among many. The Liberals attempted to reform the tax system and failed. They proclaimed a National Energy Program, designed to increase the federal government's control over petroleum resources, and succeeded; but when the price of oil plummeted in the early 1980s many saw that the cost had been great and the positive results small.

But on the constitution Trudeau prevailed. Future amendments of the Canadian constitution would be in Canada. Quebec would not have a veto over constitutional change; neither would any other single province. Language rights and, up to a point, mobility rights (the right of Canadians to move anywhere in the country and take a job without losing social welfare benefits) were entrenched, beyond the power of a province to alter. There was a charter of rights, similar to the U.S. Bill of Rights, for the first time. Although Parliament or the provincial legislatures could override the charter (the so-called "notwithstanding clause"), they had to do so specifically, publicly, and, it was hoped, embarrassingly. Surely, observers chortled, no-one would ever use it. The new constitution was proclaimed in 1982.

It was widely accepted, and according to polls, even Quebecers had no special quarrel with the new constitutional regime. The separatist government of Quebec did object, but they were, after all, separatists uninterested in making Canada work. They used the "notwithstanding clause" to exempt every single piece of Quebec legislation from the Charter of Rights, but this gesture was taken to be a sign of petulance, and temporary petulance at that, since the separatists were heading for electoral defeat in 1985, at the hands of the federalist provincial Liberals. Elsewhere in Canada, the notwithstanding clause was used only once; it proved to be deeply unpopular, and its use was believed to signify irresponsibility and a refusal to "play by the rules." Canada had moved away from parliamentary supremacy and into legal constitutionalism; the United States, of course, had made the move long before.

Trudeau's foreign policy was more mixed than his domestic record. Having partly withdrawn from Europe in 1969, he got partly back in the mid-1970s, in search of trade. Trudeau had been skeptical of the Commonwealth, but soon discovered that it was an enjoyable and relaxed place in which to argue, and perhaps, sometimes, to exert influence. It cannot be said that Trudeau ever liked NATO, but he appreciated it as a useful bridge and an occasional source of leverage on his allies. Trudeau's relations with American presidents varied. They were cool with Nixon, cordial with Ford, amiable but confused with Carter, and cool again with Reagan.

An unusual aspect of Canadian foreign policy under Trudeau derived from the federal government's strong commitment to the unity of federal states; thus, Canada supported the Nigerian federal government during the Nigerian civil war of 1969, and gave bountifully to French-speaking states in Africa lest they be tempted to give formal support to the international pretensions of the Quebec government. But it must be said that Trudeau genuinely believed in the importance of "North-South" dialogue, as between the "developed" north half of the world and the "under-developed" south, and reoriented Canadian policy to take at least some of the anxieties of the underdeveloped South into account.

In 1984 Trudeau decided his time was up, and resigned. He was briefly succeeded as Liberal leader and prime minister by one of his former ministers, John Turner. Turner reaped the resentment of all those who had been irritated by Trudeau's assertive policies, and was soundly defeated by the Progressive Conservatives under Brian Mulroney in the September 1984 general election.

Mulroney's government had an agenda very different from Trudeau's. Mulroney wanted to restore harmony to federal-provincial relations, a standard aim for any new government. He began strongly, abandoning some of the Trudeau government's policies in the energy field, thereby appeasing opinion in western Canada. Then it was time for Quebec. Mulroney owed much of his success to the support of Quebec nationalists, people who had opposed Trudeau and had largely voted "yes" (and against Canada) in that province's 1980 referendum. It was time to bring these disaffected people back into the Canadian political system, Mulroney believed, and the Liberal premier of Quebec Robert

Bourassa (elected in 1985) agreed with him. By amending Trudeau's 1982 constitutional settlement and accepting a larger role for Quebec and other provinces, by fortifying Quebec's distinct identity as a mostly French-speaking jurisdiction, this could be done. In 1986, in co-operation with Bourassa's new Liberal government in Quebec, Mulroney started negotiations that would bring Quebec "in" to the new constitution "with honor and enthusiasm." All the provinces agreed in April, 1987, at a meeting at a government resort called Meech Lake, to recognize Quebec as a "distinct society," restore its veto on constitutional amendments (by giving such a veto to everybody), and alter federal institutions to provide for provincial nominations to the Senate and Supreme Court.

Mulroney's scheme, however, became radically unhinged. It required unanimous provincial consent, by legislation in each province, and by the time some provinces got around to it, their governments had changed. The issue was mismanaged by an increasingly unpopular Mulroney government, and by the Quebec government, too. Bourassa attempted to sway English-speaking Canada by threatening, in the event of failure, to reconsider the province's position within Canada and perhaps hold a new referendum on separation. But English-speaking opinion increasingly tended to oppose the government's constitutional package, even though only two provinces, Newfoundland and Manitoba, actually rejected the deal. In June 1990 the "Meech Lake" amendments failed.

This was interpreted as a grave affront by Quebec opinion, which believed that Meech Lake was at minimum—a sign of respect and affection from the rest of Canada and long overdue. That was not how the rest of Canada saw it. Quebec's language legislation, restricting the public use of the English language on signs and in business, was seen as a deprivation of basic human rights for the province's English-language minority. When the Canadian supreme court ruled against parts of Quebec's language law, and the Quebec government subsequently over-ruled the court by using the "notwithstanding clause," Canadian public opinion was outraged. That outrage had a great deal to do with the failure of Meech Lake and the subsequent constitutional impasse in Canada,including the 1992 rejection of the Charlottetown constitutional accord by voters in English-Canada and Quebec. That accord sought to meet at accord sought to meet Quebec's demands as well as those of western Canadians and aboriginals.

The Mulroney government was active in other areas. It reformed certain aspects of Canada's tax system, although like the Reagan administration in the United States, it failed to bring the federal deficit under control: indeed, under Mulroney the deficit, and consequently the debt, grew rapidly, despite a series of tax increases. Mulroney also pursued, and eventually secured, a free trade agree-

41

ment (FTA) with the United States. He fought and won a federal election on the issue in November 1988. The free trade pact abolished tariffs between Canada and the United States over a ten year period, and also established international tribunals for regulating trade disputes between the two countries.

The free trade pact has not been without its frictions. It was unfortunate that implementation coincided with a down-turn in the North American economy. The consequent rise in unemployment in Canada was naturally blamed on the FTA. Trade did, however, increase between Canada and the United States, even in an economic recession. In terms of imports to the United States, Canada in the early 1990s ranked behind Japan and the European Economic Community; but Canada remained, by a wide margin, the principal destination of American exports.

The negotiation of free trade and its successor, the North American Free Trade Agreement (NAFTA), were not enough to salvage Prime Minister Mulroney's political career. (An attempt by his friend, President George Bush, to promote his candidacy to be secretary general of the United Nations did not attract much support internationally.) He departed office voluntarily, in June 1993, leaving his hapless successor, Kim Campbell (Canada's first woman prime minister) to suffer disaster at the next election, in October 1993. Ironically the more nationalist Liberals, under Jean Chretien, ratified NAFTA and confirmed that Canada had not the slightest intention of withdrawing from the existing free trade agreement with the United States.

Canada has been torn by the very real possibility that Quebec would choose to secede. The 1993 federal election propelled a sizeable number of separatist MPs into the national parliament, and in 1994 the separatists also won a provincial election in Quebec. The problem of government finance, expressed through Canada's high, and largely foreign-held, national debt, has also proved to be formidable. As a result, the attention of the national government increasingly centered on public finance and the reduction of government spending, even at the cost of trimming the country's social welfare policies. In addition to its economic problems, Canada has not been immune to the general trend to the right in western politics, even though, in Canada, that trend has been expressed through the country's moderate centrist party, the Liberals.

Like the United States, Canada also experienced in the 1990s a resurgence of regional feeling. With a weaker central government in Canada and much less of a world role, Ottawa had more difficulty than Washington in maintaining a strong national authority. On the other hand, thanks to the constitutional reforms of the 1980s, Canadians showed a very strong attachment to the principles, if not all the practices, of their government. Trudeau's Charter of Rights redefined Canadian nationalism. It created strong parallels to the United States, especially in terms of individual rights and an emphasis on equality. By providing a national standard in political life, it also contributed to Canadians' sense of identity. It remained to be seen whether this ideological commitment to equality would offset the centrifugal forces that called for a devolution of more and more authority to the provinces. As well, the attraction of individual, equalizing nationalism for French-speaking Canadians, with their concern for the survival of their collective language and culture, remained a very real, and politically lively, question.

It is not hard to see in these developments the contemporary representation of several predominant themes in Canadian history: regionalism or provincialism versus nationalism; French Canadian nationalism versus pan-Canadian nationalism; the attraction of the United States versus fears that Canada would be overwhelmed, at the prevailing population ratio of ten to one. It would be too much to suggest that these eternal questions will be resolved by the next Quebec referendum or even by the current generation of politicians; it is a reasonable speculation that the old questions will be around to bedevil Canadians in the twenty-first century.

## Bibliography

Bliss, Michael. *Northern Enterprise: Five Centuries of Canadian Business.* Toronto: McClelland and Stewart, 1987.

Bothwell, Robert, and William Kilbourn. *C.D. Howe.* Toronto: McClelland and Stewart, 1979.

———. *Canada and the United States.* New York: Twayne, 1992.

———. *Canada and Quebec,* Vancouver: University of British Columbia Press, 1995

Bothwell, Robert, Ian Drummond, and John English. *Canada 1900-1945.* Toronto: University of Toronto Press, 1987.

———. *Canada since 1945.* 2d. ed. Toronto: University of Toronto Press, 1989.

Brown, R.C. *Robert Laird Borden: A Biography.* 2 vols. Toronto: Macmillan, 1975, 1980.

Brown, R.C., and Ramsay Cook. *Canada, 1896-1921.* Toronto: McClelland and Stewart, 1974.

Burns, R.M. *The Acceptable Mean: The Tax Rental Agreements, 1941-1962.* Toronto: Canadian Tax Foundation, 1980.

Careless, J.M.S. *Brown of the Globe*. Vol. 2. Toronto: Macmillan, 1963.

French, R.D., and R. van Loon. *How Ottawa Decides: Planning and Industrial Policy-Making, 1968-1984*. Toronto: Lorimer, 1984.

Graham, Ron. *One-Eyed Kings: Promise and Illusion in Canadian Politics*. Toronto: Collins, 1986.

Granatstein, J.L. *Canada 1957-1967: The Years of Uncertainty and Innovation*. Toronto: McClelland and Stewart, 1986.

————. *Canada's War*. Toronto: Macmillan, 1975.

Lamb, W. Kaye. *History of the Canadian Pacific Railway*. New York: Macmillan, 1977.

Marr, William L., and Donald Patterson. *Canada: An Economic History*. Toronto: Macmillan, 1980.

McLin, Jon B. *Canada's Changing Defense Policy, 1957-1963*. Baltimore: Johns Hopkins University Press, 1967.

McRoberts, Kenneth. *Quebec: Social Change and Political Crisis*, 3rd ed., Toronto: McClelland and Stewart, 1988

Neatby, H. Blair. *The Politics of Chaos*. Toronto: Macmillan, 1972.

————. *William Lyon Mackenzie King*. 2 vols. Toronto: University of Toronto Press, 1963, 1976.

Newman, Peter C. *Renegade in Power*. Toronto: McClelland and Stewart, 1963.

Norrie, K.H. and Owram, Doug. *A History of the Canadian Economy*, Toronto: Harcourt Brace Jovanovich, 1991

Nossal, Kim R. *The Politics of Canadian Foreign Policy*, 2d ed., Scarborough, Ont.: Prentice-Hall, 1989

Owram, Doug. *The Government Generation: Canadian Intellectuals and the State, 1900-1945*. Toronto: University of Toronto Press, 1986.

————. *Canadian History: A Reader's Guide*. Vol. 2. Toronto: University of Toronto Press, 1994.

Pearson, Lester B. *Mike: The Memoirs of the Rt. Hon. Lester B. Pearson*. 3 vols. Toronto: University of Toronto Press, 1972, 1973, 1975.

Pickersgill, J.W., and D.F. Forster, eds. *The Mackenzie King Record*. 4 vols. Toronto: University of Toronto Press, 1961-70.

Pickersgill, J.W. *My Years with Louis St. Laurent*. Toronto: University of Toronto Press, 1975.

Stacey, C.P. *Canada and the Age of Conflict*. 2 vols. Toronto: University of Toronto Press, 1977 and 1981.

Statistics Canada. *Historical Statistics of Canada*. 2d ed., Ottawa: Statistics Canada, 1983.

Thompson, John H., and Allan Seager. *Canada 1922-1939.* Toronto: McClelland and Stewart, 1985.

Whitaker, Reginald. *The Government Party.* Toronto: University of Toronto Press, 1977.

Young, John. *Canadian Commercial Policy.* Ottawa: Royal Commission on Canada's Economic Prospects, 1957.